Caillou
Everything Will Be Fine

A Story About Viruses

Text: Christine L'Heureux
Illustrations taken from the animated series and adapted by Eric Sévigny

chouette   WildBrain

Caillou is at day care, playing dinosaurs with Clementine and Leo.
Anne, their caregiver, asks them to come and sit in a big circle. A very big circle.
"Children," she says. "I'd like to talk to you about something important."
Anne sounds very serious. The children are curious and listen quietly.

"Today is a very special day. A new sickness is going around. It's a bit like the flu, and it's called a virus. We have to close the day care so that the virus doesn't spread everywhere."

"Will we come back tomorrow?" asks Caillou.

Anne hesitates, then smiles.

"We don't know how long the day care will be closed. Your parents will come pick you up. Let's all get ready!"

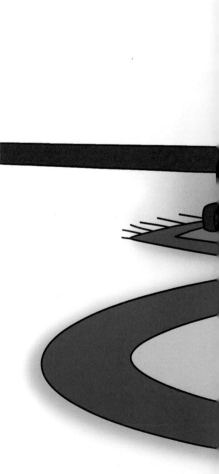

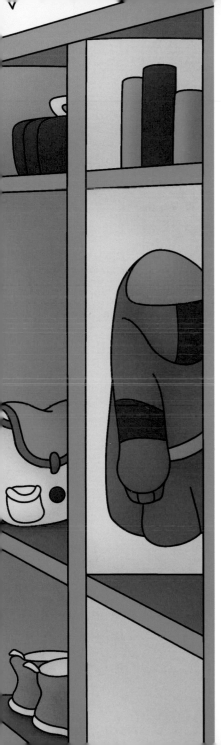

Caillou's parents arrive with Rosie.
Mommy calls to him:
"Caillou! Caillou!"
Caillou rushes into his mother's arms.
He's very happy. It's like a holiday.
"We're taking you home," Mommy says.
"Say goodbye to your friends."
"See you soon," says Caillou, waving
to Clementine and Leo.

In the car, Daddy explains:
"It's a new virus, and we don't know too
much about it. It makes you sick, and
there's no medicine to fight it yet."
Mommy adds:
"The best way to protect yourself is to
stay home, away from the virus. It's also
important to wash our hands a lot."
Caillou is very happy. Mommy and
Daddy will be with him all the time.
It'll be so much fun!

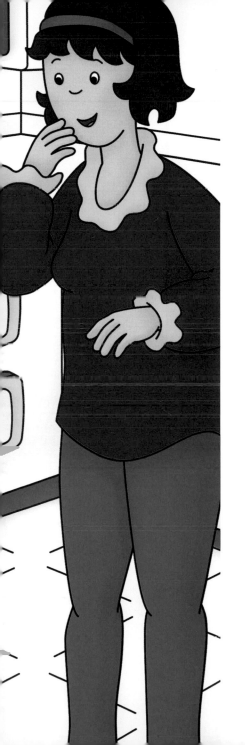

Mommy asks Caillou and Rosie to wash their hands.
"Why don't we sing a song together?" Mommy asks.
She sings:

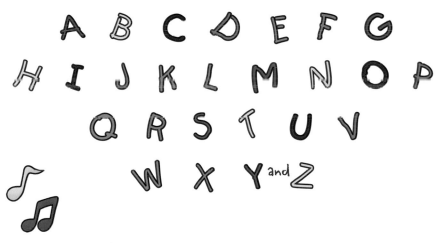

A B C D E F G
H I J K L M N O P
Q R S T U V
W X Y and Z

Now I know my ABCs
Next time won't you sing with me?

"You'll be just fine, Caillou, because you're young and healthy," Daddy explains. "But for Grandma and Grandpa, it's riskier. They're more fragile. The virus can be dangerous for older people."

"Can we phone them?" asks Caillou. Mommy calls the number, and Grandma answers.

"Grandma," says Caillou. "There's a virus outside."

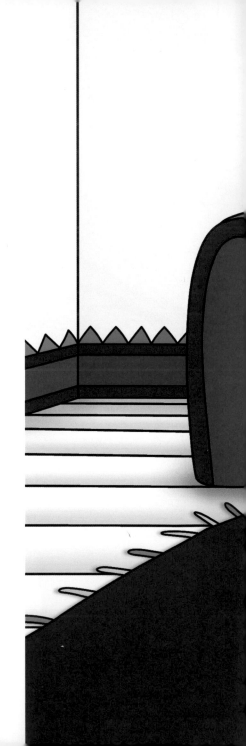

Grandma reassures Caillou:
"I'm doing very well, and we're being very careful."
Caillou asks:
"Are you going outside?"
"No," answers Grandma. "But I've started painting again and Grandpa reads a lot. He also plays his accordion."
"Don't forget to wash your hands!" says Caillou.

Caillou doesn't sleep well. In the morning, Daddy suggests, "Why don't we make a list of all the things we want to do?"
"I want to watch cartoons," says Caillou.
"Me too!" adds Rosie.
"OK," says Daddy. "In the morning, we'll get up at 7 a.m., have breakfast, and get dressed."
Mommy says, "We'll go outside to play, then we'll watch TV till lunchtime."
Caillou feels reassured. With Mommy and Daddy, it's a little bit like day care now.

Caillou is happy.

"Can we invite Clementine and Leo?"

"No," answers Mommy, "we can't see our friends so long as there's this virus."

Caillou is disappointed. He really misses his friends.

"Caillou, come with me," says Daddy.

"We'll call Clementine from my computer so you can see and talk to each other."

Caillou sees his best friend's face appear on the screen.

"Clementine," says Caillou.

"Do you want to play with me?"

"Yay!" Clementine exclaims.

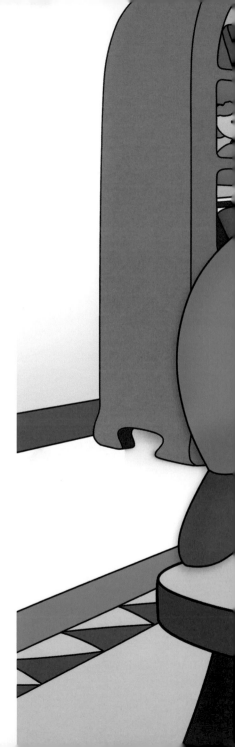

"Hello, Clementine," says Daddy. "Caillou still has the costume from your show at day care. He can dress up as the sun. What about you?"

"Yes!" shouts Clementine. "I have my flower costume."

"Why don't you both put on your costumes?" says Mommy. "What kind of story can we make up?"

Caillou and Clementine are having fun! It's like being at day care.

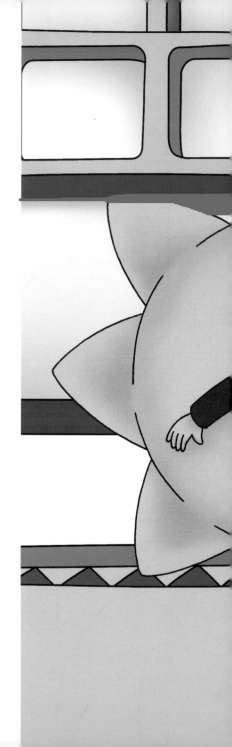

Mommy asks Caillou and Rosie to wash their hands.
"Let's sing together."
She sings:

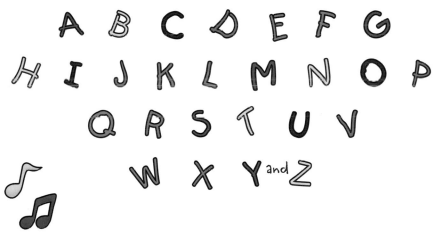

A B C D E F G
H I J K L M N O P
Q R S T U V
W X Y and Z

Now I know my ABCs
Next time won't you sing with me?

Text by Christine L'Heureux
All rights reserved.
Illustrations taken from the animated series and adapted by Eric Sévigny
Coloration: Eric Lehouillier

The PBS KIDS logo is a registered mark of PBS and is used with permission.

Chouette Publishing would like to thank the Government of Canada and SODEC
for their financial support.

Bibliothèque et Archives nationales du Québec and Library and Archives Canada
cataloguing in publication

Title: Caillou: everything will be fine: a story about viruses / Christine L'Heureux; illustrations,
Eric Sévigny.
Other titles: Caillou: ça va bien aller. English | Everything will be fine: a story about viruses
Names: L'Heureux, Christine, author. | Sévigny, Éric, illustrator.
Series: Clubhouse
Description: Series statement: Clubhouse | Translation of: Caillou: ça va bien aller.
Identifiers: Canadiana (print) 2020007962X | Canadiana (ebook) 20200079409 |
ISBN 9782897186036 (softcover) | ISBN 9782897186005 (EPUB) |
ISBN 9782897186012 (PDF)
Classification: LCC PS8573.H49 C3513 2020 | DDC jC843/.54—dc23

Legal deposit – Bibliothèque et Archives nationales du Québec, 2020.
Legal deposit – Library and Archives Canada, 2020.

Printed in Canada
10 9 8 7 6 5 4 3 2   CHO2107 AUG2020